Rejoice Together

Prayers, Meditations, and Other Readings for Family, Individual, and Small-Group Worship

Edited by Helen R. Pickett

Skinner House Books
Boston

Printed in the USA.

ISBN 1-55896-298-0

10 9 8 7 6 5 4 3 2 1
99 98 97 96 95

Acknowledgments

Every effort has been made to trace the owner(s) of copyright material. We regret any omission and will, upon written notice, make the necessary correction(s) in subsequent printings.

Permission to use the table grace and the Christmas reading by Percival Chubb, an Ethical Culture Leader in the American Ethical Union, was granted by the American Ethical Union, Copyright © 1955. The American Ethical Union Library Catalog number 54:11625.

Algerian and Columbian prayer from the UNICEF Book of Children's Prayers, edited by William I. Kaufman. Copyright © 1970 by William I. Kaufman. Reprinted by permission of the author.

The lines from "The Invocation to Kali" are reprinted from A Grain of Mustard Seed, New Poems by May Sarton, by W.W. Norton & Company, Inc. Copyright © 1971 by May Sarton.

"A Man's Prayer" by Robert R. Walsh is from Noisy Stones. Copyright © 1992 by Robert R. Walsh. Reprinted by permission of the author.

Contents

Introduction

Unitarian Universalists worship in many different ways. The word "worship" comes from the Middle English "worshipe", meaning worthiness. We worship, then, whenever we ascribe worth or worthiness to some value, idea, object, person, experience, attitude, or activity, or whenever we give form or shape to that which we have already found to be of worth.

A worship experience can occur at any time, whether one is alone or part of a group. Whenever something beautiful is perceived, whenever there is a deep sense of connectedness with other persons, with the natural world, or with the transcendent (however defined), whenever one gains insight or a new sense of wholeness, whenever one perceives an ethical challenge, whenever life is deliberately focused or ordered—all of these situations may be considered worship.

In 1990, the Unitarian Universalist Church of the Larger Fellowship published the *Handbook of Religious Services,* a collection of readings and meditations to help laypersons plan and conduct simple worship services or special ceremonies in family or small group settings.

Rejoice Together provides a broader selection of readings for worship and is designed to be used as a self-contained worship or meditation resource, or as a supplement to the *Handbook of Reli-*

gious Services. The book is divided into two main sections, one primarily for families and intergenerational groups, the other for small, lay-led groups. Most of these materials were gathered from Unitarian Universalist sources, including the UUA's hymnbook, *Singing the Living Tradition*. I want to express special thanks to the contributors for permitting me to use their work.

Helen R. Pickett

I

Family Worship

Some 200 years ago, when Unitarianism and Universalism were new in North America, prayers were part of the family's daily ritual. Gradually, we have let go of this practice. Though some UU families still say grace at meals or encourage children to say bedtime prayers, even these simple customs have been largely abandoned.

Some form of religious observance—call it worship, celebration, or what you will—is necessary to our spiritual growth whether we're part of a congregation or not. We may worship, celebrate, sing, and meditate by ourselves when we feel the need. We may also create opportunities to do these things together as a family in our own home.

In the *Handbook of Religious Services*, the Rev. Robert L'H. Miller wrote:

> The stuff of your daily life experience and its language and style of expression should provide content and context for family celebrations. Our celebrations affirm our beliefs in the goodness of life, the supreme worth of persons, the creative process of sharing, the search for truth. Our celebrations clarify our values and help us to learn what is good, what kind of person am I, what kind of persons are others? Our celebrations enhance our feeling

of fellowship, oneness, awareness of traditions, family roots, and heritage, a sense of freedom to speak, think, and participate.

How can Unitarian Universalist families, especially those who do not live near a UU congregation, create our own occasions for religious observance? Here are some ideas and suggestions to stimulate your creativity.

Around the Dinner Table
Try to find at least one time during the week when the whole family can sit down for a meal together. It may turn out to be a weekend breakfast instead of an evening meal. If you gather regularly around the dinner table, you have more opportunities for the simple observances that can make the time together meaningful for all.

Lighting a Chalice or a Candle
You can make your own chalice by placing a small votive candle in a shallow bowl. When you sit down together, take turns lighting the chalice and saying special words. You'll find suggestions in this booklet. Or simply say:

Today, I'm thankful for . . .
This flame is to help us remember . . .
Today, I'm thinking about . . .
This day is important to me because . . .

Saying Grace
Suggested table graces are also given in this booklet. Or your family can collect lines of poetry or other readings that are meaningful to you. Take turns saying grace in your own words, or hold hands around the table for a silent grace, passing around a hand-squeeze to say "Amen."

Celebrating Milestones and Special Occasions

Birthdays, of course! In addition to your usual practices, add a few minutes to reflect on the past year and share favorite memories of, by, or about the birthday person, ways in which she/he has grown or wishes and hopes for the coming year.

Seasons of the year are natural points of celebration. The first days of spring, summer, autumn, and winter, or special days such as Ground Hog Day, May Day, Halloween, or All Saints Day (a good Universalist holiday!) are some examples.

Birthdays of Famous Persons

Choose a "famous birthday" to celebrate each month. Let various members of the family be responsible for decorations, food, and appropriate stories, readings, or songs. If a cake with candles makes it Happy Birthday time at your house, then do it for Thomas Jefferson and Clara Barton as well!

Creating a Setting

You can do any of the following:

- After eating, clear the table and place a chalice, candles, flowers, or special objects on it.
- Form a half circle of chairs around the fireplace, perhaps adding a special picture on the mantelpiece.
- Spread a brightly colored cloth on the floor, arranging bits of nature or art around your chalice in the center. Sit around in a circle.
- Gather outdoors in a beautiful spot.

Creating a Pattern

Here is how one family gathers for a Sunday morning service in their living room:

- Each member of the family lights a candle.
- Opening words are said. You can use a selection from this

booklet, a favorite poem, or something appropriate from a newspaper, magazine, or book.

- Recorded music is played.
- Thoughts for the week are said. Each person shares high points and low points of the past week, what they are looking forward to in the coming week, and anything they are worrying about.
- Closing words are said, or a song they sing together.
- Each member takes a turn doing the opening words and choosing the music.

Other Ways to Create a Service Together

Set up a box or paper bag in which you can drop ideas or themes for services as they occur to you, for example, P. T. Barnum's birthday, the Harvest Moon, helping others, making your home ecologically responsible, or Black History Month.

After your family worship, but while you are still gathered in your worship space, someone reaches into the box or bag and pulls out a slip of paper with a theme. Decide as a group who is to be responsible for creating a visual focal point, opening words, a song, a reading, and a closing. Agree to present this service the next time you gather.

You might also plan a service around religious questions that members of the family raise. (Do we believe in Jesus? What happens when people die? Why do bad things happen?) Take some time to gather ideas and materials that focus on the question in different ways. Encourage other members of the family to say how they feel about the question or what their responses might be. The point, of course, is not so much to answer the question as to give it the attention and importance that it deserves and to keep those big questions coming.

Whatever pattern of religious celebration you develop, make it your own, enjoy it, and keep it flexible so that it can grow and change. Worshipping together can enrich your experience of life and deepen your relations with one another.

The prayers and readings in this section were selected to help you create a special time for your family.

Opening Words

Many of the past generation and many today have found
   three abiding values in prayer:
   the quiet meditation on life,
   the reaching out toward the universal and the infinite,
   and the courageous facing of one's profoundest wishes.
Let parents sense and share with their children the glory
   and mystery of everyday things.
Let them look with sympathy upon humanity's age-long
   dilemmas.
Let no questions be taboo.
The next generation can ill afford to have the deeper values
   deleted from the book of life.

SOPHIA LYON FAHS

Into this place may we come
   to share,
   to learn,
   to speak,
   to listen,
and to grow together in the spirit of peace and harmony
   and love.

FRANCES REECE DAY

It is a blessing to be.
It is a blessing to be here.
It is a blessing to be here now.
It is a blessing to be here now, together.

SOURCE UNKNOWN

Everybody wake up!
Open your eyes! Stand up!
Be children of the light—strong, swift, and sure of foot.
Hurry, clouds, from the four quarters of the universe.
Come, big snows, that water will be abundant this summer.
Come, ice, cover the fields, that the seeds may grow into
    good crops.
All hearts be glad!

Our lives are made up of small moments:
    sharing a meal with friends or family,
    wondering about a question that puzzles us,
    giving help to another,
    listening to a person and being listened to,
    talking with another about something that makes us sad,
    an embrace, a smile, a touch,
    offering a thought that might help, just a little, to make
        more sense of it all.
Our gathering here is just such a small moment.
It is a small thing we do in gathering. Yet it is significant.
May we affirm and celebrate the moments that we share
        here today.

BRUCE MARSHALL

Children all,
We come together
In faith and hope,
To find what meaning life holds for us,
To laugh and sing with one another,
To soothe the wounds of daily life,
And to grow together in wisdom and love.

MARJORIE C. SKWIRE

Words for Chalice or Candle Lighting

[In unison]
Flaming chalice, burning bright,
now you share with us your light.
May we always learn to share
with all people everywhere.

EVA M. CESKAVA, ADAPTED

We light this candle to remind ourselves to treat all people
kindly, because they are our brothers and sisters.
We light this candle to remind ourselves to take good care
of the earth, because it is our home.
We light this candle to remind ourselves to live lives full
of goodness and love, because that is how we will become
the best men and women we can be.

SOURCE UNKNOWN

For every time we make a mistake
and we decide to start again,
we light this chalice.

For every time we are lonely
and we let someone be our friend,
we light this chalice.

For every time we are disappointed
and we choose to hope,
we light this, our chalice.

M. MAUREEN KILLORAN

We light this chalice for the light of truth.
We light this chalice for the warmth of love.
We light this chalice for the energy of action.

MARY ANN MOORE

Prayers and Meditations

For flowers that bloom about our feet,
for tender grass so fresh and sweet,
for song of bird and hum of bee,
for all things fair we hear or see,
    Giver of all, we thank you.

For this new morning with its light,
for rest and shelter of the night,
for health and food, for love of friends,
for everything your goodness sends,
    Giver of all, we thank you.

RALPH WALDO EMERSON

I have seen the waters flow in the river.
I have seen the flowers along the banks of the river.
Passing by, I have gazed upon the countryside
    and inhaled the perfume of the orange blossoms.
I have been grateful to God and I have said thank you.

ALGERIAN PRAYER

Help us to be the always hopeful
Gardeners of the spirit
Who know that without darkness
Nothing comes to birth
As without light
Nothing flowers.

MAY SARTON

Whatever road I take
    joins the highway
    that leads to God.
Broad is the carpet God has spread
    and beautiful are its colors.

PERSIAN

I praise the blue sky.
I praise the sun that is in you.
I praise the bright moon.
I praise the shining stars in you.

SOURCE UNKNOWN

God of life and beauty:
We pray for the quietness of snowflakes, knowing that love
    is quiet.
We pray for the kindness of small acts, knowing gentleness
    is fragile.
We are grateful to know that thoughtfulness makes no sound,
    that compassion leaves wonderfully beautiful traces
    when we open ourselves to wonder.
May ours be a religion which, like the snowflake, goes
    everywhere in quietness, in love, and with gentle
    regard for that which is true and beautiful,
    in us and about us. Amen.

LUCINDA STEVEN DUNCAN

Give me beauty in the inward soul,
and may the outward and the inward me be at one.

SOCRATES

Great Spirit, fill us with light.
Give us the strength to understand and eyes to see.
Teach us to walk the soft earth as relatives to all that live.

SIOUX PRAYER

May we have eyes that see, hearts that love,
and hands that are ready to serve,
for we would take our part as good neighbors in this wide world.

SOURCE UNKNOWN

To this quiet place of beauty
we have come from workday things,
pausing for a while and waiting
for the thoughts that quiet brings.

SOURCE UNKNOWN

At a Time of Loss

Eternal Spirit, whom we call God,
    you are our life.
You are the best and the most beautiful in us and beyond us.
Your spirit is in animals, birds, plants, and in people
    whom we do not know or who seem very different from us.
All of us share the gift of life.
Help us to remember that life is good.
Help us to know that we don't stop loving people or other living
    things when they are no longer close to us.
Love lasts always.
May we look for ways to love one another, and to love
    all living things. Amen

LUCINDA STEVEN DUNCAN

Source of all life:
We celebrate life's beauty; we are a part of life's joy.
We know that both life and death are real.
We never would choose to part with one we have loved,
    but whenever there is great love, there is great
    memory, a great understanding that we carry in
    ourselves the best of the life that is gone.

May we show our love and celebrate the life remembered
in our daily small kindnesses and give thanks for the love
that we share. Amen.

LUCINDA STEVEN DUNCAN

This sparrow (puppy) died today,
this feathered (furry) creature small.
We lay it in the friendly Earth,
which holds and shelters all.

SOURCE UNKNOWN

Table Graces

For all we eat, for all we wear,
for all good things everywhere,
we thank you, God. Amen.

SOURCE UNKNOWN

Earth, who gives to us this food,
Sun, who makes it ripe and good:
Dear Earth, dear Sun, by you we live;
to you our loving thanks we give.

NATIVE AMERICAN

May we have grateful hearts, and may we be mindful of the needs
of others. Amen

SOURCE UNKNOWN

God, we thank you for this food,
for rest and home and all things good,
for wind and rain and sun above,
but most of all, for those we love.

SOURCE UNKNOWN

For health and strength and daily food, we give you thanks,
O God. Amen.

SOURCE UNKNOWN

Here at the table now we pray:
    keep us together day by day;
    may this, our family circle, be
    held fast by love and unity.

JOHN S. MACKEY

In the light of love and the warmth of this family
we gather to seek, to sustain, and to share. Amen.

SOURCE UNKNOWN

A circle of friends is a blessed thing.
Sweet is the breaking of bread with friends.
For the honor of their presence at our table
    we are deeply grateful. Amen.

SOURCE UNKNOWN

We lift our hearts in thanks today
for all the gifts of life.

PERCIVAL CHUBB

The food that we are about to eat
    is the fruit of the labor of many beings and creatures.
We are grateful for it and bless it.
May it give us strength, health, and joy,
    and may it increase our love as a family/for each other/
    for the human family.

JOHN R. B. SZALA

For bread, for friends, for joy and sorrow, for the comfort of
quietness, let us ever be grateful and caring.

RUDOLPH W. NEMSER

May we hold hands quietly for a moment . . . ,
feeling love flow around us and through us,
knowing that as we give love away
there is always more within.

SOURCE UNKNOWN

Bedtime Prayers

*The following suggestion is taken from a letter written by Christopher Gist
Raible to a seven-year-old girl who had asked, "What prayer shall I say when
I go to bed?"*

Think of prayer as an honest expression of some of your
feelings, especially three kinds of feelings. Sometimes you
feel thankful for nice things that have happened to you. If
you express your thanks at bedtime, you may enjoy them
all over again. Sometimes you feel sorry for things that
you have done or said. If you express your feeling of being sorry before you go to sleep, you may feel much better. Sometimes you have hopes for yourself and other
people. If you express your hopes in prayer, you may see
what you can do to make them come true.

Each night you could make up your own prayer. It could
begin "Tonight I am thankful for . . ." and then you could
think of some of the most important things you are thankful for. It could continue "Tonight I am sorry for . . ." and
then you could think of some of the most important
things you are sorry about. Your prayer could then end

with "Tomorrow I hope . . ." and you could think of some of the most important things you hope for and think how you can help to bring them about.

I am thankful for the night
and for the pleasant morning light,
for health and strength and loving care
and all that makes the world so fair. Amen.

SOURCE UNKNOWN

Give me, O God, your blessing
before I give myself to sleep;
and while I slumber,
watch over all those I love. Amen.

COLOMBIAN PRAYER

Thank you, God, for all life brings,
for health and play and all good things,
and help me use my heart and mind
to make me strong and keep me kind. Amen

ROBERT M. AND
POLLY C. COOPER

Readings

Who can be certain where the self stops and the universe
    begins?
When we breathe, it is the air from the passing wind that
    fills our lungs.
To our nostrils drifts the fragrance of the woodland flower.
When we taste, it is of the earth's flavors and its saltiness.
When we eat, it is of the field's corn and its wheat.

When we open our eyes, they are filled with sunlight and
    starlight.
Who can be certain where the self stops and the universe
    begins?

TODD J. TAYLOR

To Our Children

We wish for you a storm or two that you may enjoy the
    calm.
We wish for you tranquility in time of trial.
We wish you a cool breeze on a warm day, and pale white
    clouds that you may better appreciate the blueness of
    the sky.
We wish you darkness that you may see the stars.
We wish you anticipation of high adventure, and we wish
    you the courage to avoid battle.
We wish you a sense of wonder—and poetry—and music.
We wish you companionship that you may appreciate
    solitude.
We wish you a friend who will understand you, and under-
    standing so that you may have a friend.
We wish you may become all that you wish to be, and more
    than you hope that you can be.
We wish you a flower to smell,
A hand to touch
A voice to cheer
A heart to gladden
And we wish you someone to love, as we love you.

ROBERT F. KAUFMANN

Peace means the beginning of a new world; peace means a whole world like one country. It means that nations are friends; it means joy to the world.

Peace is quiet and calm; it is rest; it is silence after a storm. It is love and friendship; it is the world's dream of dreams.

It means that the strong respect the weak, the great respect the small, the many respect the few. Peace brings comfort and happiness; it brings bread to the hungry; it brings prosperity to nations.

Peace is like a mother to those who have suffered; peace after war is like sleep after a long journey. It is like spring after winter; it brings sunshine into the world; it is like sweet music after harsh sounds.

PUPILS OF THE LINCOLN SCHOOL,
NEW YORK CITY (ARRANGED)

We believe
that each and every person is important,
that all people should be treated fairly and kindly,
that we should accept one another and keep on learning
    together,
that each person must be free to search for what is true and
    right in life,
that all persons should have a vote about the things that
    concern them,
in working for a peaceful, fair, and free world,
in caring for our planet earth, the home we share with all
    living things.

UNITARIAN UNIVERSALIST PRINCIPLES, FROM *WE BELIEVE*

Closing Words

May the peace of flowing water be with us;
may the beauty of starry skies be with us;
may the warmth of companionship be with us;
and may the miracle of this world in its fullness bless us this
    day and each day of our lives.

MARYELL CLEARY

I am only one. But still I am one.
I cannot do everything, but still I can do something.
And, because I cannot do everything, I will not refuse to do
    the something that I can do.

EDWARD EVERETT HALE

Let us go forth from this place ready to
    extend a hand to others,
    open our hearts in sharing, and
    find kind words of praise for all we meet.

ALEXANDER MEEK, JR.

As we leave this friendly place,
love give light to every face;
may the kindness which we learn
light our hearts till we return.

VINCENT SILLIMAN

Group Worship

When Unitarian Universalists gather for worship, they intend to create some kind of shared and worthwhile experience. A worship service is a deliberate shaping, ordering, or recalling of individual thoughts and experiences, done in the context of a community of persons who share common values, ideas, and attitudes.

Just as important as the content of any worship service is the setting created by the worship leader/s. Many non-verbal dimensions of the worship experience can directly affect the quality of the service. Here are a number of suggestions that can ensure a rewarding worship experience for everyone involved.

Creating a Setting

First, arrange whatever space is being used to ensure that it looks and feels like "sacred" space—space that reflects the worth and beauty of what is being celebrated, cherished, affirmed, or embraced.

First Impressions Are Important
Is the worship space clean, neat, and cared for? Is it bright, welcoming? Are the chairs and other furniture thoughtfully and pleas-

ingly arranged? Is the lighting comfortable? (Sometimes soften-
ing the lighting just as the service begins is very effective.) Does
the worship space reflect the care and concern you have for your
Unitarian Universalist faith? A little attention to such physical
details can make a world of difference!

Starting On Time
Beginning on time reduces the discomfort of visitors and com-
municates to everyone that you are well organized and serious
about the service. Some UU groups use a gentle gong, a bell, or
soft prelude music to let people know that the service is about to
begin and that it is time for them to take their seats and prepare
themselves for worship.

Order of Service
Provide an Order of Service for participants to follow. It can be
printed ahead of time and handed out, or posted in front of the
group. A printed Order of Service helps participants relax because they know that they do not have to worry about being
surprised or confused during the service. If the group regularly
recites or sings something together, make sure the words are
printed for visitors.

A Focal Point: Art Objects, Symbols, Decorations
When you arrange the room to draw attention to a central point—
perhaps adjacent to a podium, lectern, or pulpit—you enhance
the experience of comfort, community, inspiration, and sense of
purpose that shared worship can bring. Simplicity is usually the
key to effective use of flowers, paintings, sculpture, or banners. If
possible, find an object that is related to the day's theme; it can
be enjoyed in itself and provide a symbolic reinforcement for the
theme. Symbols are particularly well suited to worship because
they invite viewers to ponder their personal responses.

Greenery or Flowers
Live plants or flower arrangements can add greatly to an atmosphere of peace, reflection, serenity, and beauty. Place them carefully to complement other worship-space objects (chalice, symbols, banners).

The Flame of Fellowship
The ritual lighting of a candle or chalice at the start of a service can become a powerful and meaningful symbol to focus group worship. You may do this with or without spoken words.

Music
Music can bring about religious and spiritual experiences that words cannot. Music evokes moods of celebration and contemplation, amplifying and intensifying the spoken word. Live music has excitement and immediacy, but recorded music, if carefully selected and skillfully presented, can also be effective. Group singing invites active participation in the service.

Congregational Participation
Merely by their presence, individuals who come to worship are participating. In addition, participation can be formalized by communal activities: hymns, unison and responsive readings, and affirmations; sharing announcements, personal joys, concerns, and prayers; a feedback time after the service or presentaton, or questions and dialogue structured into the service. As a rule, some structured participation enriches worship for the congregation, but services can be effective without it. Varying the forms of congregational participation can prevent "staleness" and offer additional levels of engagement for those who attend.

Putting the Service Together

Spend some time identifying and focussing on the theme of your service. Perhaps there is a seasonal holiday, an event of significance in the community, an ethical, political, or religious controversy, or a personal perspective you wish to address. A clear focus is essential.

Gather Materials
Make an outline of the components you envision in your service. With a general plan in mind, choose readings, meditations, music, and other elements that you feel enrich your theme or focus.

Prepare Service Copy
Make copies of your selected materials so that you can arrange them in the order in which you will present them. Prepare a copy of the entire service with all elements in their proper order, and place it securely in an attractive folder or binder.

Final Preparations
When you have the whole service organized, read it through carefully. Note any special materials you may need to have on hand (candles, lighters, flowers), or people who must be contacted to take part (pianist, ushers). Practice reading the service aloud at a slow, measured pace—people not trained as public speakers often speak much too rapidly. Ask someone to listen and comment on your delivery.

Review the steps for setting the stage, plan for your focal point, and decide how to print or display an Order of Service. Make a checklist of all the things that must be taken care of by you or someone else before the service begins. When you have tended to these details, you are ready! Take a deep breath and proceed.

If you wish to consult some additional resources for planning and conducting Unitarian Universalist worship, the following are available from the UUA Bookstore, 25 Beacon Street, Boston, MA 02108:

Handbook of Religious Services
Singing the Living Tradition
The annual UUA meditation manuals

You may also request a free UUA Bookstore catalogue for a list of other worship resources.

Opening Words

We come together now to worship.
Spirit calls to spirit.
Hand reaches out to hand.
Heart joins with heart.
Voice lifts with voice a song of praise.
Come, let us worship together.

CALVIN O. DAME

These are the days that have been given to us;
    let us rejoice and be glad in them.
These are the days of our lives;
    let us live them well in love and service.
These are the days of mystery and wonder;
    let us cherish and celebrate them in gratitude together.
These are the days that have been given to us;
    let us make of them stories worth telling to those who come
        after us.

WILLIAM R. MURRY

Welcome
    to a day of hope and promise,
    to a place of peace and comfort,
    to a journey toward truth and justice,
    and to a community of love and courage
    that will help us along the way.

ANITA FARBER-ROBERTSON

We come together to celebrate who we are, to share the in-
    sights that give meaning and hope to our lives, to learn
    from the wisdom of others, that their truths may con-
    tribute to our understanding.
We gather, we share, we learn; we celebrate our coming together.

ANN PEART

Amid all the noise in our lives,
we take this moment to sit in silence—
    to give thanks for another day,
    to give thanks for all those in our lives who have brought us
        warmth and love,
    to give thanks for the gift of life.

Let us open ourselves, here, now,
to the process of becoming more whole—
    of living more fully,
    of giving and forgiving more freely,
    of understanding more completely the meaning of our lives
        here on this earth.

TIMOTHY D. HALEY

Welcome to this time of seeking and finding, for it is in our
coming together here that we celebrate who we are and who
we yet shall be.

JANE ELLEN MAULDIN

We come together today seeking a reality beyond our narrow
selves that binds us in compassion, love, and understanding to
other human beings, and to the interdependent web of all
living things.

May our hearts and minds be opened to the power and the
insight that weave together the scattered threads of our experience and help us remember the Wholeness of which we are a
part.

WAYNE B. ARNASON

Come, let us worship together.

> Let us open our minds to the challenge of reason,
> open our hearts to the healing of love,
> open our lives to the calling of conscience,
> open our souls to the comfort of joy.
>
> Astonished by the miracle of life,
> grateful for the gift of companionship,
> confident in the power of living faith,
> we are here gathered.

Come, let us worship together.

LINDSAY BATES

Welcome to this place of possibility!
This is love's hearth, the home of hope,
> a refuge for minds in search of truth unfolding, ever beautiful,
> > ever strange.
Here, compassion is our shelter,
> freedom our protection from the storms of bigotry and hate.
In this place, may we find comfort and courage.
Here may our sight become vision to see the unseen,
> to glimpse the good that is yet to be.

MARIANNE HACHTEN COTTER

In this time we turn our thoughts to how we can
> touch and be touched,
> love and be loved,
> forgive and be forgiven,
> heal and be healed,
so that the goodness of our lives is a shared blessing.

MARTA M. FLANAGAN

Welcome to this place.
Here we seek justice and truth.
Here we celebrate life and contemplate mystery.
Here we find healing and wholeness.
Welcome.

RAYMOND R. NASEMANN

We summon ourselves from the demands and delights of
        the daily round
    from the dirty dishes and unwaxed floors,
    from unmowed grass and untrimmed bushes,
    from all incompletenesses and not-yet-startednesses,
    from the unholy and the unresolved.

We summon ourselves to attend to our vision
    of peace and justice,
    of cleanliness and health,
    of delight and devotion,
    of the lovely and the holy,
    of who we are and what we can do.

We summon the power of tradition and the exhilaration
        of newness,
    the wisdom of the ages and the knowing of the very young.
We summon beauty, eloquence, poetry, music to be the
    bearers of our dreams.

We would open our eyes,
    our ears,
    our minds,
    our hearts
to the amplest dimensions of life.

We rejoice in manifold promises and possibilities.

GORDON B. McKEEMAN

Let there be joy in our coming together.
Let there be truth heard in the words we speak and the
    songs we sing.
Let there be help and healing for our disharmony and
    despair.
Let there be silence for the voice within us and beyond us.
Let there be joy in our coming together.

CARL SEABURG

Fling wide the windows, O my soul!
The bright beams of morning are warm.

We pause in reverence before the wonder of life,
    the wonder of this moment,
    the wonder of being together, so close yet so apart,
    each hidden in a secret chamber,
    each listening, each trying to speak,
    yet none fully understanding,
    none fully understood.

We pause in reverence before all intangible things
    that eyes see not, nor ears can detect,
    that hands can never touch,
    that space cannot hold,
    and time cannot measure.

Fling wide the windows, O my soul!
The bright beams of morning are warm.

SOPHIA LYON FAHS

May our souls be united in praise and wonder
    for that which remains still amid the flow;
    for that which remains quiet amid the music;
    for that which remains cool amid the heat;

for that which remains dark amid the blaze;
for that which remains alive amid death;
for that which remains while all is changing.
For all these let us give thanks and praise.

W. FREDERICK WOODEN

We stop. We pause. We pay attention. We center ourselves.
We free ourselves from the compulsion of projects to finish,
    work to be done, things to accomplish.
We leave ourselves alone for a time.
We journey deep down into that quiet center where no
        voice is heard.
We live for a brief time on an island of peace.
We apprehend the world from a quiet center.
Here is the center of the world.
In this instant are centered the whirling orbs, the movement of
    earth and sky.
In this fragile moment of time is the culmination of all that has
    been and the promise of all that shall be.
Here in our grasp, in this moment, is the center of the
        world.

RICHARD S. GILBERT

We gather this day; we come in search of life's meaning.
All of us have moments of weakness and times of strength;
    all sing songs of sorrow and love.
May our worship bring us strength along our way.
In the presence of the sacred, may we come to know our true
    selves, finding a fresh impulse to love and do good.

MARTA M. FLANAGAN

This hour is sacred because we make it so!
By our presence with each other we renew our bonds.
Let us join together in compassion and understanding to seek
wisdom.
Let us turn aside from transient cares and contemplate anew the
enduring mystery that is life.
Let us open ourselves to receive the gifts of love and peace.

JIM WICKMAN

All that quickens sympathetic imaginings,
all that awakens sensitivity to others' feelings,
all that strengthens courage,
all that adds to the love of living—
belongs to us.
May our spirits be quickened and enriched, strengthened and
enhanced by our being here together.

GEORGE G. BROOKS

For untold centuries people have drawn apart from the worka-
day world to worship, to celebrate, and to wonder at things
beyond and within themselves.
So we are gathered here to raise our sights and look at new
horizons. Life is more than toil for bread; life has meaning and
purpose.
As we celebrate life together, let us seek harmony within
ourselves, with one another and the world, and find our lives
uplifted and made whole.

MARYELL CLEARY

A day,
yes, another day—
this day is ours:
its beauty, its promise,
its weight of sorrow and disappointment,
the brightness of its opportunity for doing and achieving,

of its opportunity for the deepening of love and understanding.
This day is ours, even as we make it ours
by the readiness and warmth of our appreciations,
for from it we shall receive according to the measure of our
     giving.
Let our giving be of ourselves, and from the heart.
May there be laughter in this day, and if there be tears, then
     generous tears.
Another day?
Ah, yes—a day.

VINCENT SILLIMAN

For Seasonal Celebrations and Special Occasions

FOR ANY SPECIAL OCCASION

When love is felt or fear is known,
when holidays and holy days and such times come,
when anniversaries arrive by calendar or consciousness,
when seasons come, as seasons do, old and known, but some-
     how new,
when lives are born or people die,
when something sacred's sensed in soil or sky,
mark the time.
Respond with thought or prayer or smile or grief.
Let nothing living, life or leaf, slip between the fingers of the
     mind,
for all of these are holy things we will not, cannot, find again.

MAX A. COOTS

EASTER/SPRING

Today we come, as people have come for thousands of years,
    to worship and sing praises,
    to celebrate the victory of hope over despair,
    to be reminded of the ever renewing life of the spirit,
    and to mark the season of springtime come again.
Welcome to our festival of joy!

POLLY LELAND-MAYER

May we be united in praise and wonder.
Let us bless this moment that, though brief, is precious to
      eternity.
Let us bless the hour, that it is given us to shape and for us to
    be shaped by.
Let us bless the day, that it is new and yet familiar, fresh and
    yet venerable.
Let us bless the season, that it is fragrant with flowers and loud
    with insects.
Let us bless the power that pours forth moments, hours, days,
    weeks, months, years, in careless generosity, much as
    dandelions and mosquitos spill out in May.

W. FREDERICK WOODEN

SUMMER

Let us rejoice in the light of this day,
in the glory and warmth of the summer sun, and
in the blooming and bursting of new life.
Let us rejoice in the earth with its grass and trees,
its weeds and flowers, its many fruits and hidden treasures.
Let us rejoice together this day.

CONNIE STERNBERG

THANKSGIVING

We gather this morning in the spirit of thanksgiving:
    we give thanks for this family/fellowship,
    for the bounty of this season,
    for beauty of earth and sky, and of human creations,
    for love, given and received.
Let us make our thanks for these blessings manifest in our words
    and in the warmth of our companionship.
Let us say "thanks" to Life!

MARYELL CLEARY

CHRISTMAS

Invocation in the Spirit of Christmas
(In tribute to the spirit of Charles Dickens)

[*Responsively*]
In the Spirit of Christmas Past,
let us gather to listen and learn
the ancient stories,
    THAT OUR HEARTS MAY FIND WISDOM.

In the Spirit of Christmas Present,
let us gather to view and question
the way things are,
    THAT OUR HEARTS MAY SEEK JUSTICE.

In the Spirit of Christmas Future,
let us gather to dream and to plan
the way things will be,
    THAT OUR HEARTS MAY BE RECLAIMED BY HOPE.

LAURALYN W. BELLAMY

Welcome, rich season of bounty and good cheer! Wreathe every life with garlands of innocent mirth. Crown with green wreaths of joy the brows of those we love; weave in red berries of health, and the bright star of hope.

Welcome, blest season of peace, that brings a truce to strife! And may your white wings of peace spread over the waiting earth. Link all peoples and nations in the sure bonds of community; shed peace and good will, good will and peace, on all humanity.

PERCIVAL CHUBB

We are the ones who keep Christmas. Christmas is what we want it to be. Christmas is loveliness, happiness, singing, laughter, giving, and sharing, if we will make it so.

May this season be a time of rebirth and renewal, a time of happiness and joy. Let there be light and warmth, and let us be their bearers.

JEANNE H. M. BELL

For a Service of Memory and Hope

We pause this hour to remember
    those whom we have lost,
    those whom we fear losing,
    those from whom we are separated,
    those to whom we would extend a helping hand, a caring
        heart, the will to live.
We pause this hour also to hope
    for life and good living,
    for love and kind words,

for reconciliation,
for the support of family and friends,
for meaning in our struggle,
for wholeness.
May our memories and hope renew us for the days and nights
       to come.

M. SUSAN MILNOR

Words for Chalice or Candle Lighting

Glory be to the earth and the wind.
Glory be to the sun and the rain.
Glory be to animals and children
    and women and men.
Glory be to our holy flame
    which calls us together as one.

BETTYE A. DOTY

We light this chalice to celebrate the love within us, among us,
and all around us.

DAVID HERNDON

May this light kindle within us
    the warmth of compassion
    the glow of love
    the fire of commitment
    the light of truth.

MARIANNE HACHTEN COTTER

May this flame be
    as the light of wisdom in our minds
    and as the warmth of love in our hearts.

HAROLD E. BABCOCK

May unity and peace abide within us.
May wholeness and joy touch our hearts.
May kindness and compassion fill our universe
    and reverence fill our days.
May we see the light that shines in all.

GARY KOWALSKI

We light the flame of knowledge;
    may understanding be with us.
We light the flame of love;
    may caring be among us.
We light the flame of holiness;
    may the unifying spirit be within us.

EDWIN C. LYNN

This flame glows
    as light glows in the darkness.
This flame dances
    as growing things dance upon the green earth.
This flame flickers
    as life flickers for a precious while in each of us.
This flame is warm
    as the companionship of family and friends is warm.

ANDREW M. HILL

As others before us have sought to make ordinary
    times special by lighting a candle,
we now seek to transform this ordinary time
    into a special and sacred one
by lighting the flaming chalice, symbol of our faith.

PENNY HACKETT-EVANS

In flame from this chalice
we find the light of faith,
    the glow of hope,
    and the warmth of service.
May we ever grow in faith, hope, and service
as we kindle our own lights from its spark.

WAYNE B. ARNASON

To face the world's coldness,
    a chalice of warmth.
To face the world's terrors,
    a chalice of courage.
To face the world's turmoil,
    a chalice of peace.
May its glow fill our spirits, our hearts, and our lives.

LINDSAY BATES

We light our flaming chalice
to illuminate the world we seek.
In the search for truth, may we be just;
in the search for justice, may we be loving;
and, in loving, may we find peace.

ELIZABETH McMASTER

May the flame here lit
be to us a symbol of the torch
that is passed from hand to hand, and life to life—
of caring and concern and the passion for involvement
which have marked the men and women of our liberal faith
for many generations.

PHILIP R. GILES

As the polestar once guided explorers,
may the flame of this chalice guide us
to ever better understandings of
ourselves and our universe.

NORMAN V. NAYLOR

We drink from wells we did not dig.
We have been warmed by fires we did not build.
We light this chalice in thanksgiving
for those who passed their light to us.

ROBERT SCHAIBLY

For centuries people have told stories, celebrated life, and
approached the ultimate while gathered around a fire.
Today we light this chalice
    that the hearth fire of our hearts may be rekindled,
    that our stories may be retold,
    that we might celebrate life anew, and
    that we might approach what is of ultimate value.

DENISE D. TRACY

Let the lighting of the chalice remind us that we can recognize
the value of light only when we know, as well, the importance
of darkness. So, as we celebrate the awakening, the visual
delights, and the opportunity to find our way that the morning
brings, we also give thanks for the rest, repose, and renewal
that are the potential gifts of the night.

PETER WELLER

May this flame,
symbol of transformation since time began,
    fire our curiosity,
    strengthen our wills, and
    sustain our courage
as we seek what is good within and around us.

BETS WIENECKE

The light of this chalice is a frail thing.
It can be snuffed out by the winds of cynicism and apathy.
May its little flame be a reminder of the power of the spirit.
Let us rededicate ourselves to providing light that lifts
    our hearts and increases the world's joy.

ALAN G. DEALE

We see the chalice light.
Let it symbolize today
    the light within.
Let it shine today
    through each one of us,
    in the way we feel
    and in what we do.
Let the light shine.

ROBERT M. DOSS

This flame affirms the light of truth, the warmth of love, and
the fire of commitment.

[*As the flame is extinguished at the end of the service, these words may be
said:*]

We extinguish this flame but not the light of truth, the warmth
of love, or the fire of commitment which it here symbolizes.
These we carry in our hearts until we come together again.

ELIZABETH SELLE JONES

May the lighting of this flame renew in us our endless
    search for all that is right and true,
our abiding love of life and all who share this life,
and our unending dedication to following paths of peace
    and justice.

ELIZABETH B. STEVENS

We gather this hour as people of faith
with joys and sorrows, gifts and needs.
We light this beacon of hope, sign of our quest
for truth and meaning,
in celebration of the life we share together.

CHRISTINE ROBINSON

For Seasonal Celebrations and Special Occasions

CHILD DEDICATION

We light this chalice in wonder and appreciation for the gifts of
childhood, and we dedicate ourselves to the nurture of those
gifts, that our children may grow in beauty and in love.

CONNIE STERNBERG

SPRING/PASSOVER/EASTER

We light our chalice to remember the sorrow, the loss, and the
    joy that are within this season of the year.
The Passover, that brought freedom from slavery and bondage
    for the Jewish people, continues to bring light into the world.
Palm Sunday, Good Friday, and Easter, that brought joy and
    the triumph of life over death for the Christian people,
    still bring the light of that joy to the world.

The spring equinox, that brings new life bursting forth on the
    land each year, brings lengthened days of sunlight to all
    life.
Passover for freedom, Easter for life, spring for rebirth.
We light our chalice for all three.

ELIZABETH M. STRONG

We light this chalice as a symbol of our thankfulness.
The chalice reminds us of the sun, the giver of life.
The flame rises up like the power of growth and renewal in the
    springtime.
We give thanks
    for the sun, which lights and warms the earth,
    for the growth and renewal of nature, arising from the
        earth, and
    for the earth itself.

DAVID J. MILLER

SUMMER

As we light this chalice, we are glad of summer light that wakes
color in the world so early and keeps it up so late.

We are glad of the light of the mind that does not depend upon
the time of day, the time of year, or the time of life to enlighten
us and to beckon us inward, outward, and onward in exploration of the many realms of being.

We are glad of the light of the heart that accompanies us in our
search for companionship in life, for worthy work to do, and for
ways to overflow in joy and in deeds of courage and compassion.

Let us rejoice in the many glad meanings of light.

GRETA W. CROSBY

THANKSGIVING

For daylight and darkness,
for sunshine and rain,
for the earth and all people,
we offer deep thanksgiving.
We kindle this light in celebration
of the life that we share.

GARY KOWALSKI

May the goodness of the earth continue to sustain us.
May the goodness of friends and family continue to support us.
May the joys of this holiday renew us.

KATHERINE W. INGLEE

CHRISTMAS

Into the bright circle of life and light which is the Christmas
season we have come, to warm our hearts and minds at the
cradle of the child.

May something of the beauty, mystery, and promise of this
lovely old story fall like silver rain upon the broken dreams, the
hates and fears of all.

Once again may we pause, look up, and in the far-off distances
hear that old, old music, the music of hope, brotherhood,
sisterhood, and blessed peace!

ALFRED S. COLE

May the candle/s we light this holiday season remind us of the
glowing love within the heart. May the carols we sing uplift
our spirits and renew our hope and vision. May the special

moments we spend with family and friends strengthen the bonds of caring between us at this time and throughout the coming year.

PATRICK GREEN

GRIEF/LOSS

In our time of grief, we light a flame of sharing, the flame of ongoing life. In this time when we search for understanding and serenity in the face of loss, we light this sign of our quest for truth, meaning, and harmony.

CHRISTINE C. ROBINSON

Prayers and Meditations

As we sit here quietly, we are aware of our connections with each other in this room; we are aware of our connections with people of faith all around the world; we are aware of our connections with all of nature—in fact, the universe itself. May we truly experience and appreciate our interdependence with all of life.

RODNEY E. THOMPSON

O God, whom we know as Love,
help us to recognize the love that surrounds us and in which we
    have our being.
Help us to see ourselves as the loving people we are and can be.
In silence, now, we bring to our mind's eye the people who have
    loved us and continue to love us,
        people who are not here with us today, but whose love we
            carry with us,
        people who are there every day, and whose love we some-
            times take for granted,

people who might be within our circle of love, could we
    but extend it a little further.
In silence, now, we hold these people in our hearts. [*Silence*]
In returning from silence, we ask that our hearts may be opened to
    all whose names and faces have crossed our minds and that the
    love we share with the people in our lives may be our
      abiding teacher.

WAYNE B. ARNASON

We give thanks for the earth and its creatures
    and are grateful from A to Z:
for alligators, apricots, acorns, and apple trees;
for bumblebees, bananas, blueberries, and beagles;
coconuts, crawdads, cornfields, and coffee;
daisies, elephants, and flying fish;
for groundhogs, glaciers, and grasslands;
hippos and hazelnuts, icicles and iguanas;
for juniper, jackrabbits, and junebugs;
kudzu and kangaroos, lightning bugs and licorice;
for mountains and milkweed and mistletoe;
narwhals and nasturtiums, otters and ocelots;
for peonies and persimmons and polar bears;
quahogs and Queen Anne's Lace;
for raspberries and roses;
salmon and sassafras, tornadoes and tulipwood;
urchins and valleys and waterfalls;
yaks and yams and yogurt.
We are grateful, good Earth, not least of all,
for zinnias,
zucchini,
and zebras,
and for the alphabet of wonderful things
that are as simple as ABC.

GARY KOWALSKI

Let us be quiet, without and within.
Let the stillness be in us.
Let the silence hold us.
May we find the deep places of the soul and begin to let go of the
    distractions which plague us.
May we let go of irritation, calm the confusion which inhibits us,
    let go of fear.
The quiet is within us.
The stillness is in us.
The silence will hold us.
There are deep places in the soul.
Here, may we find peace.

HAROLD E. BABCOCK

For simple things that are not simple at all:
    for miracles of the common way—
        sunrise, sunset,
        seedtime, harvest,
        hope, joy, ecstasy;
    for grace that turns
        our intentions into deeds,
        our compassion into helpfulness,
        our pain into mercy;
    for Providence that sustains and supports our needs,
we lift our hearts in thankfulness,
    and pray only to be more aware
    and thus more alive.

GORDON B. McKEEMAN

I wonder if the river ever despairs of its downward destiny and
    harbors a secret desire to flow up.
I wonder if winter yearns to be summer, or if a flower wishes it
    could bloom out of season.
I wonder if silence would like to shout, or if the sky wants to
    fall down and become the earth.

I wonder if the bird longs to become a rabbit, or if the fish ever
  dreams of walking on the land.
I wonder if the mountains envy the valleys, or if snow secretly
  covets the warmth of June.
I wonder if the moon complains that it is not the sun, or if the
  stars envy the earth.
I wonder if rain prefers a cloudless sky, or if grass tires of
  green and hopes for blue.
I wonder if spring really likes growing, or if fall rages against
  its colorful dying.
I wonder if the world ever sighs after more than it is—as we do,
  as we do.
O Spirit of Life, we struggle against our limitations. Teach us to
  accept them.

BURTON D. CARLEY

Holy and Creative Light, teach us to love this Earth, our home.

Together we live in one small house, even though to us it seems
so large and with so many rooms. This quiet planet, marbled
blue and white, was hanging here and spinning in black space
long before we came. Whole families, kingdoms, empires of
teeming life arose and passed away before us. Now we are here,
not knowing how or why.

Slowly we have begun to learn about our house: how delicate,
how self-contained, how easily torn apart! Holy it is, this
bubble of rock, water, air—not to be consumed nor smashed
like the toy of a careless child, but to be cared for and cherished, to be kept clean and liveable for all the later tenants in
their generations.

Teach us to be servants of life, not prideful masters. For we are
caretakers and stewards here, with this great responsibility: to

watch over the house, to savor its beauty, to breathe its air.

CHARLES GRADY

Eternal God, Mother and Father, Spirit of Life,
We are grateful for the companionship of hearts and minds
    seeking to speak the truth in love.
We are grateful for our heritage, for the women and men before us
    whose prophetic words and deeds make possible our
    dreams and our insight.
We are grateful for the gift of life itself, mindful that to
    respect life means both to celebrate what it is and to insist
    on what it can become.
May we always rejoice in life and work to cultivate a sense of its
    giftedness, but may we also heed the call to transformation
    and growth.
May we find in ourselves the strength to face our adversities, the
    integrity to name them, and the vision to overcome them.
May we honor in pride the heroines and heroes of our past, but
    may we also keep company with the fallen, the broken, and
    the oppressed, for in the dazzling of noonday's heat, and in
    the star-studded shimmering of night's rich blackness, we
    are them.

M. SUSAN MILNOR

Words tell us of our thoughts,
silence helps us hear our deeper feelings.

In silence, we sense the rhythmic measures of all life
in the slow repetitive rhythm of our own bodies.

In silence, we feel the ebb and flow of life's breath
as the waves of the larger ocean in which we all live.

In silence, we sense a larger spiritual presence of which we are
all a part.

In silence, we sense the coming and going of human pathways, knowing we can ask no more than to have reached out to others in creative and caring ways.

And in this silence, we know it is this human touch that gives the larger journey its meaning.

EDWIN C. LYNN

Knowing that we do not always live up to our best expectations of ourselves, let us in quietness seek the good within, which some call the Inner Light, and some "a spark of the divine."
[Silence]
Knowing that we live in a society that falls far short of the ideal, let us in quietness resolve to do one thing this week to aid those suffering from want and injustice.
[Silence]
Knowing that the earth is our home and that humankind is making it a dirty and even poisonous home, let us in quietness consider how we might be part of making it more healthful for all living things.
[Silence]
Knowing that each of us has some sorrow or worry hidden within, let us consider in quietness how we may reach out to one another with our smiles, our handclasps, and our encouraging words.
[Silence]

MARYELL CLEARY

Let us pray to the God who holds us in the hollow of His
    hands, to the God who holds us in the curve of Her
    arms,
to the God whose flesh is the flesh of hills and hummingbirds and
    angleworms,
whose skin is the color of an old black woman and a young

50

white man, and the color of the leopard and the grizzly
    bear and the green grass snake,
whose hair is like the aurora borealis, rainbows, nebulae,
    waterfalls, and a spider's web,
whose eyes sometimes shine like the Evening Star, and then like
    fireflies, and then again like an open wound,
whose touch is both the touch of life and the touch of death,
and whose name is everyone's, but mostly mine.
And what shall we pray?
Let us say, "Thank you."

MAX A. COOTS

Simply to be, and to let things be as they speak wordlessly
    from the mystery of what they are,
simply to say a silent yes to the hillside flowers, to the trees
    we walk under,
to pass from one person to another a morsel of bread, an
    answering yes, this is the simplest, the quietest, of sacraments.

JACOB TRAPP

Let us reflect for a few moments in silence.

As Unitarian Universalists we believe that each individual is
free to determine what is finally good and right and true, and
that freedom carries with it the responsibility for each of us
honestly and vigorously to seek out life's deeper meanings. So
let us remind ourselves that our quest is neither trivial nor
inconsequential, but of primary concern, if we are to live well
and fully.

Therefore, let us reflect on the ways in which each of us feels
called upon to change and grow. And let us resolve that in the
days and weeks to come we may live closer to that ideal.

Let us reflect for a few moments in silence upon the possibilities for our lives.

DOUGLAS GALLAGER

Forgive us that often we forgive ourselves so easily and
        others so hardly;
forgive us that we expect perfection from those to whom
        we show none;
forgive us for repelling people by the way we set a good
        example;
forgive us the folly of trying to improve a friend;
forbid that we should use our little idea of goodness as a
        spear to wound those who are different;
forbid that we should feel superior to others when we are only
        more shielded;
and help us to appreciate the secret struggle within every
        person.

VIVIAN POMEROY

Let this house be quiet.
Let our minds be quiet.
Let the quietness of the hills,
the quietness of deep waters,
be also in us:
So quiet that the noise
of passing events and present
anxieties,
of random recollections
and wandering thoughts,
is stilled;
So quiet that the marvelous
stillness is like music;
So quiet that we feel
the very being which is
the life of us all;

So quiet that we are renewed,
we feel at one with all others,
at home in a tabernacle
of stillness;
So quiet that we sense
the ripples of this pool
of quietness and healing
pass through us and out
to the farthest star.

JACOB TRAPP

In an unsettled world, we seek for a few moments to turn away
from the noise and confusion of our lives. We seek to enter a
stillness, a stillness that resides in the depths of each of us, a
stillness that is at the center of all that exists.

For a few moments, let us seek quiet—not the quiet that is the
    absence of noise, for there is always noise.
Rather, it is like the stillness of a friend listening,
    the noontime silence of sunlight on a lake,
    the silence of a new idea, a thought that makes
        the world pause,
    the quiet of growing plants,
    the quiet of a child sleeping,
    the silence that brings rest,
    the silence that brings renewal,
    the silence from which hope and love emerge.

Let us pause for a few moments, to listen for the stillness that
rests beneath the confusion and complexities of our lives.
[*Silence*]

BRUCE T. MARSHALL

O Thou, whose kingdom is within,
may all thy names be hallowed.
May no one of them be turned against the others
to divide those who address thee.

May thy presence be made known to us
in mercy, beauty, love, and justice.
May thy kingdom come to be in the life
of all humankind.
May it come with peace, with sharing,
and in a near time.

Give us this day our daily bread,
free from all envy and alienation,
broken and blessed in the sharing.

Keep us from trespass against others,
and from the feeling that others are
trespassing against us.
Forgive us more than we have forgiven.

Deliver us from being tempted by lesser things
to be heedless of the one great thing:
the gift of thyself in us.

THE LORD'S PRAYER,
ADAPTED BY JACOB TRAPP

The friendship we share this day is sacred.
    All gatherings when people meet and touch,
    celebrate life.
The laughter we share this day is sacred.
    Joy and sorrow that rise from love
    are springs of life.
The stillness we share this day is sacred.

In this peace is a haven for the spirit
that nurtures life.
For friends, for joy and sorrow, for the comfort of quietness,
let us ever be grateful and caring.

RUDOLPH W. NEMSER

For Seasonal Celebrations and Special Occasions

THE NEW YEAR

Eternal Spirit,
God of light and darkness,
at this time of year,
when days are short and nights are long,
as we take stock of life,
as we reflect on success and defeat,
allow us an awareness of how far we have come.
Remind us of friends and family who remain
steadfast and dear to us.
Remind us to bundle together and keep warm
within our family/community.
Rejoice with us in our accomplishments
and mourn with us our losses.
Help us to make workable resolutions and goals,
knowing that our personal lives touch
and influence the lives of others.
Give us perspective to make priorities.
Be with us, Eternal Spirit,
as we render designs and draw blueprints
for the year to come.
So be it.

JUDITH SMITH-VALLEY

SPRING/EASTER

We are waiting for the sun to show its strength. The winter is too long, and spring seems to trifle with us. The everyday cold has made us tired, our neighbors and children and co-workers tired. We are waiting to rise from the dead.

Who is not ready for the poetry of spring: the forsythia that blooms overnight, the digging, the surprise of the lengthening day?

May we savor the air as it grows warmer and easier to breathe. May we love the earth again, and while we wait once more for the sun to show its strength, may we care for one another.

JANE RANNEY RZEPKA

O Mystery!

O mystery beyond my understanding,
Voice in my heart answering to the earth,
And light of distant stars!
O wonder of the spring, leading the seasons on:
The dewdrops sparkling on the web at sunrise,
And unseen life, moving in depths and shallows of the brook,
Trembling in raindrops at the edge of eaves,
Whisper to me of secrets I would know.
O Power that flows through me and all that is,
Light of stars, pulsating in the atoms in my heart,
Whether you are mind and spirit
Or energy transcending human thought
I cannot know, and yet I feel
That out of pain and sorrow and the toil
Through which creation springs from human hands
A force works toward the victory of life, even through the stars.

Here on the earth winter yields slowly, strikes again, and hard,
And lovely buds, advance guards of the spring, suffer harsh
    death,
And pity moves the heart.
Yet life keeps pulsing on.
The stars still shine, the sun rises again,
New buds burst forth, and life still presses on.
O mystery!
I lift my eyes in wonder and in awe!

ROBERT T. WESTON

MOTHER'S DAY/FATHER'S DAY

As we come together, may we find cessation of whatever
    personal turmoil accompanies us.
May we seek forgiveness for harsh words uttered, or healing
    words left unsaid.
May each of us find strength to endure difficulty;
    may we find acceptance of those we may not understand.
And, as this season becomes more glorious with each passing
    day, may we be aware of each and every miracle around us,
    and be glad!
On this day when custom reminds us to remember those who
    gave us life and nurtured our early years,
let us give deep thanks for each person, female or male, family
    or friend, who loved and guided us to be who we are today.
May we find ways to express that love in words and in the
    ongoing integrity of our lives.
And let us be supporters of each other in this uncertain
    venture that is our shared life, that our lives may be
    strengthened and enriched.

POLLY LELAND-MAYER

AUTUMN

For the beauty of the autumn,
   brilliant skies,
   pale asters,
   dogwood leaves veined with purple,
   smell of dusty decay not to be found another time,
let us be thankful.

For places of peace and strength,
   sanctuaries of holiness,
   communities of caring,
   times of thought, listening silences,
let us be thankful.

For what we have to be held and shared,
   bread,
   wisdom,
   warmth,
   love mysteriously reaching another being,
let us be thankful.

RUDOLPH W. NEMSER

THANKSGIVING/EARTH DAY/FLOWER COMMUNION

Dear God of earth and sky,
of polluted streams
and birds that cry,
today we celebrate and remember
   to care for the earth,
   to clear its waters,
   to purify its air,
   and replenish its soil
which feeds us fruitfully.

God of earth and sky,
of singing streams
and birds that fly,
we celebrate and give thanks
today
and all our
tomorrows.

JEAN WITMAN GILPATRICK

THANKSGIVING

In quiet that deepens into silence
we move from
the surface of sound and the spoken word
to rest in deeps from which springeth all sound,
as a flower trembling
at the edge of living.
Hear our cry, God of the silence,
and hear our laughter.

Signs and sounds of gratitude
tremble into being
as we labor:
the hammer blow is thanks,
and the knotting of a thread, and
listening expectantly at the edge of sound.

All things are thanks and the giving of thanks.

THEODORE A. WEBB

O God, when we thank you for what is given to us and not to
        others,
    let us remember to pray softly, for there will be many who
        will overhear.

Let conscience search our gratitude! This bounty did not come
        to us because, more than others, we are deserving.
O God of Truth, rebuke us—until the needy multitudes press in
        upon our prayers.
These are our sisters and brothers! We are one family.
O God, to whom we bring our gratitude, help us to remember
        the many who will overhear!

A. POWELL DAVIES

Eternal God, source of all created things, we would give
        substance to our thankfulness by resolving to make
        right use of the gifts we have received from your
        bounty.
With your gift of the senses we would fashion and preserve
        a world of beauty for all.
With your gift of reason we would engage in a responsible
        search for truth.
With your gift of compassion we would build a world of
        justice and mercy.
And with your gift of Being we would walk together in
        peace.
Thus, in gratitude, may we become faithful servants of your
        glorious ongoing creation.

ROBERT R. WALSH

WINTER

The Snow Drifts Down

Across the hill and dell, valley and upland,
Smooth as a blanket across the world,
Softly falling, falling,
Quietly, gently as a mother's kiss

On the face of her sleeping child,
The snow drifts down, touches, settles,
Lies on tree and shrub, on field and woodland,
Like a soft mantle,
Making all things new.
So be my heart this day:
The pain of things done and injuries unmended,
The fears of things unseen and long dreaded,
The ache of failures and mistakes of times past,
The sudden angry passion and the bitter regret,
And strength ebbing away with the inexorable beat of time—
All forgotten, or restored to innocence,
Clothed in gentle purity,
The universal forgiveness which whispers to me,
"Behold, I make all things new!"

ROBERT T. WESTON

CHRISTMAS

Gifts that matter have no weight.
They are without substance.
Gifts that matter most are given to us by the Hand of Life
     in grace:
    moonlight on fresh-fallen snow,
    frost delicately etched on a window pane,
    crackling fireside, bright because of who is there,
    aromas of cooked food betokening a family feast,
    reunion of those long separated,
    memories of Christmas past, gone but not forgotten,
    anticipations of the new year yet to be,

gift-givers whom we love,
  the gift of life itelf.
Gifts that matter have no weight.

RICHARD S. GILBERT

Readings

Some beliefs are like walled gardens. They encourage exclusiveness and the feeling of being especially privileged. Other beliefs are expansive and lead the way into wider and deeper sympathies.

Some beliefs are divisive, separating the saved from the unsaved, friends from enemies. Other beliefs are bonds in a universal humanity, where sincere differences beautify the pattern.

Some beliefs are like blinders, shutting off the power to choose one's own direction. Other beliefs are like gateways opening wide vistas for exploration.

Some beliefs weaken a person's selfhood. They blight the growth of resourcefulness. Other beliefs nurture self-confidence and enrich the feeling of personal worth.

Some beliefs are rigid, like the body of death, impotent in a changing world. Other beliefs are pliable, like the young sapling, ever-growing with the upward thrust of life.

SOPHIA LYON FAHS

A Man's Prayer

I am wondrously wrought: partly shaped by my biology, partly shaped by my culture, and partly self-shaped.

I am so wondrously fashioned that the workings of my self amaze and confuse me.

I know I have the power to choose among many paths in life, yet most of the time I am on automatic pilot, acting out of little-examined assumptions, values, rituals, myths, appetites, and impulses.

I can meet life in many ways:
I can be tough-minded; I can be tender-hearted.
I can move between activity and quietness.
I can express my uniqueness and individuality, and I can forget myself in commitment to family and community.
I can judge, I can bear witness to the good and evil around me; and I can forgive.
I can analyze, theologize, figure the world out; and I can listen to the still small voice of conscience, intuition, holy spirit.

All these ways of meeing life, and more, are part of the potential that is me. But I am afraid to move very far or very fast from the ways that have become comfortable.

I seek the self-knowledge that may illuminate new possibilities in life, and I seek the courage to try them.

Most of all I pray for wholeness, for a life in which my many ways of living can be connected and filled with the meaning of holy Creation.

ROBERT R. WALSH

We are always dancing, often delicately and with difficulty, on the twin horns of dilemma. In most instances of human conflict, both horns are in some way true. It is their truth that creates the dance, and it is in this very dance that we are free. Whenever an idea reigns unchallenged by another point of view, there is no freedom because there is no choice.

Thus, conflict is the cost of freedom. If we treasure choice we may also learn to honor conflict and discover it may grant us peace and strength and stature. In devotion to the cause of freedom, disagreement may indeed unite us.

MARGARET A. KEIP

Deep in our selves resides the religious impulse.
Out of the passions of our clay it rises.
We have religion when we hold some hope beyond the
 present, some self respect beyond our failures.
We have religion when our hearts are capable of leaping up
 at beauty, when our nerves are edged by some dream in
 the heart.
We have religion when we have an abiding gratitude for all
 that we have received.
We have religion when we look upon people with all their
 failings and still find in them good; when we look
 beyond people to the grandeur in nature and to the
 purpose in our own heart.
We have religion when we have done all that we can, and
 then in confidence entrust ourselves to the life that is
 larger than ourselves.

RALPH N. HELVERSON

To laugh
    is to risk appearing the fool.
To weep
    is to risk appearing sentimental.
To reach out for another
    is to risk exposing our true self.
To place our ideas, our dreams, before the crowd
    is to risk loss.
To love
    is to risk not being loved in return.
To hope
    is to risk despair.
To try
    is to risk failure.
To live
    is to risk dying.

ANONYMOUS

I wish for the dull a little understanding, and for the understanding a little poetry. I wish a heart for the rich and a little bread for the poor. I wish some love for the lonely and some comfort for the grieved.

I wish companionship for those who must spend their evenings alone. I wish contentment for the aged, who see the days slipping by too quickly, and I wish dreams for the young. I wish strength for the weak and courage for those who have lost their faith. And I wish we might all be a little kinder to each other.

FRANK SCHULMAN

Death is not too high a price to pay
for having lived. Mountains never die,
nor do the seas or rocks or endless sky.
Through countless centuries of time, they stay
eternal, deathless. Yet they never live!

If choice there were, I would not hesitate
to choose mortality. Whatever Fate
demanded in return for life, I'd give,
for, never to have seen the fertile plains
nor heard the winds nor felt the warm sun on sands
beside the salty sea, nor touched the hands
of those I love—without these, all the gains
of timelessness would not be worth one day
of living and of loving; come what may.

DOROTHY N. MONROE

Two travelers on their way to Japan were standing at the rail of
the ship looking out upon the vast open sea. After but a few
moments, one of the men turned about and walked away,
disappointment written on his countenance. Throughout the
day, the man returned to the deck rail and then turned his back
upon the scene, each time appearing more disconsolate than
before.

Finally the second traveler, who had remained at the rail, felt
compelled to ask his fellow traveler what it was that made him
so downcast on what was evidently a pleasure trip. The first
man replied that he had been told that at this point of the
voyage he would be able to see Mt. Fuji rising in the distance.
However, the haze over the water was apparently not going to
lift, depriving him of a sight that he had so long anticipated.

Taking him by the arm, his shipmate led the man back to the
rail of the ship and said quietly, "Look higher." The traveler,
raising his eyes above the haze, saw, in all its beauty and
majesty, the great mountain peak.

ANNE BOWMAN, ADAPTED

Last night, in the hour just before the dawn, I awoke to hear the familiar "honk" of the wild geese somewhere up there in the murk of the October night. Whether they were on their trek to the southland, I do not know, but the honk awakened within me (as it always does) a sense of wonder, something elemental and deep in the heart of life, calling from the skies. What is it that guides them through the night to their destination? It fascinates me.

We are children of earth also. Is there something in our highest moments that draws us toward our goals? In the realm of the spirit does this call, which urges the wild goose to go south-ward, also move and impel us onward—this something at the heart of things? This is the wonderment that seizes my heart during the southward flight of birds.

ALFRED S. COLE

Often I have felt that I must praise my world
for what my eyes have seen these many years,
and what my heart has loved.
And often I have tried to start my lines:
    "Dear Earth," I say,
    and then I pause
    to look once more.
    Soon I am bemused
    and far away in wonder.
So I never get beyond "Dear Earth."

MAX A. KAPP

For Seasonal Celebrations and Special Occasions

THE NEW YEAR

A Year Begins Today

A year is gone.
It matters not when it began
For it has ended now.
There were other years,
And some began with a birthday
And some with a death;
Some with one day of the month and some with another.
Some began with a song and others with a lament,
But today I start another year, whatever the month or season;
It is what lies before me that concerns me now.
There will be decisions and tasks;
There will be drudgery, achievement, and defeat:
There will be joy and grief.
All the raw stuff of experience
Waiting for me to shape, to fashion as I will,
And it will never become just what I planned.
However it may appear to others
I can turn it to knowledge and wisdom
Or folly.
If it be hard, I can make of it strength:
It may become bone, sinew, and steel
Or ashes and waste.
Someone might say, "It all depends on what the year may
    bring,"
But what I make of it depends on me.

ROBERT T. WESTON

SPRING/EASTER

Here is a day of promise!
May it be so with me, with every one!
The gray clouds scudding overhead,
The storm clouds, rain, and the breaking sunshine,
The apple blossoms bursting in pink and white,
The children gleefuly running out to splash in puddles,
The grass green, and the buds
Straining into leaves on shrubs and trees,
And the birds singing, joyfully, in the dawn,
Strutting the lawns as proud possessors.
Everywhere life, life bursting through all fetters,
And the heart singing, protesting against gloom,
Shouting its defiance of clouds and cold;
The gay heart exulting in storm and sunshine alike.
This is a day that aches with the promise of life,
Life which will not be denied.
Let all hearts swell with glad acceptance,
Joyful with the sense of the always becoming,
For out of earth, into the air and sunshine, out of ourselves,
There rises spirit in us,
Neither dark nor threat shall thrust it down.
It rises irresistible in us.
This is the season's gift.

ROBERT T. WESTON

Jesus is risen from the dead.

The centuries have not been able to bury him.

Forsaken by friends,
sentenced to die with thieves,
his mangled body buried in a borrowed tomb,

he has risen to command
the hearts of millions, and
to haunt our hate-filled world
with the restlessness of undying hopes.

The years bring him increasingly to life.
The imperial forces that tried to destroy him
have long ago destroyed themselves.
Those who passed judgment upon him
are remembered only because of him.

Military might and political tyranny
still stalk the earth;
they too shall perish,
while the majesty of the carpenter-prophet
bearing his cross to the hill
will remain to rebuke the ways of violence.

CLINTON LEE SCOTT

THANKSGIVING

Epilogue

Now is the time to live; now is the time,
As nature may disclose, to savor life:
To know its streams, its woodland hills to climb,
To read its cliffs, engraved with ancient lore,
To share its moods, the carefree and sublime,
And thrill with beauty from its ancient store.

Now is the time, in wonder to explore
From whisp'ring tree and softly answering dove
To storied shells beside the storm-swept shore,

From starflower to the galaxies above:
Then shall peace flood the restless heart once more
As autumn beauty fills the woods we love.

Now is the time to live, to look, to see,
To taste that life is good, to share its zest
And know its patience in the dormant tree,
The budding earth, the motion that is rest;
Creation in each moment flowing free
Nor dread the sunset in the dark'ning west.

ROBERT T. WESTON

WINTER

Let us not wish away the winter. It is a season in itself, not
simply the way to spring.

When trees rest, growing no leaves, gathering no light, they let
in sky and trace themselves delicately against dawns and
sunsets.

The clarity and brilliance of the winter sky delight. The loom
of fog softens edges, lulls the eyes and ears of the quiet, awakens by risk the unquiet. A low dark sky can snow, emblem of
individuality, liberality, and aggregate power. Snow invites to
contemplation and to sport.

Winter is a table set with ice and starlight.

Winter dark tends to warm light, fire, and candle; winter cold
to hugs and huddles; winter wants to gifts and sharing; winter
danger to visions, plans, and common endeavoring—and the
zest of narrow escapes; winter tedium to merrymaking.

Let us therefore praise winter, rich in beauty, challenge, and pregnant negatives.

GRETA W. CROSBY

CHRISTMAS

For so the children come
and so thay have been coming.
Always in the same way they come—
born of the seed of man and woman.
No angels herald their beginnings,
no prophets predict their future courses.
No magi see a star to show where to find the babe that will
    save humankind.

Yet each night a child is born is a holy night.
Parents, sitting beside their children's cribs,
feel glory in the sight of a new life beginning.
They ask, "Where and how will this new life end?
Or will it ever end?"

Each night a child is born is a holy night,
a time for singing,
a time for wondering,
a time for worshipping.

SOPHIA LYON FAHS

They told me that when Jesus was born, a star appeared in the heavens above the place where the young child lay.

When I was very young I had no trouble believing wondrous things; I believed in the star. It was a wonderful miracle, part of a long ago story, foretelling an uncommon life.

They told me a super nova appeared in the heavens in its dying burst of fire.

When I was older and believed in science and reason, I believed the story of the star explained.

But I found I was unwilling to give up the star, a fitting symbol for the birth of one whose uncommon life has been long remembered.

The star explained became the star understood, for Jesus, for Buddha, for Zarathustra.

Why not a star? Some bright star shines somewhere in the heavens each time a child is born. Who knows what it may foretell? Who knows what uncommon life may yet again unfold, if we but give it a chance?

MARGARET K. GOODING

Christmas is more than a date in the calendar.
Christmas is a mood, a sentiment, a symbol.
It is the quickening of the presence of other persons
    into whose lives we have invested a part of our own lives.
It is a memory of other days when into one's path
    a special one appeared to turn an ordinary moment
    or a commonplace event into a hallowed experience.
Christmas is home and hearth, the full, free laughter of children,
    the remembrance of friends, and a moment of peace
    amid the noisy conflicts within and without.
It is a gathering up of the transcendent dreams of the centuries,
    signalized in the birth of a child
    who became the Prince of Peace.
Christmas is a time when goodwill is reborn, and again made real
    in the hopes and hearts of us all.

CLINTON LEE SCOTT

Closing Words

May the quality of our lives
be our benediction
and a blessing to all whom we touch.

PHILIP R. GILES

May the spirit of truth and love
rule our hearts and minds
and guide us into those ways
that will create love, justice,
and peace on the earth.

RICHARD M. FEWKES

A Friend Along the Way

Dare we look into one another's eyes
and discover there a friend?
Dare we lower our masks and confess
our humanity is flawed
and still profess
compassion for one another?

In whose spirit do we congregate?
Or why do we bother
to struggle and celebrate
our common life?

Perhaps it is in recognition
of this truth that we sustain:
no matter who we are or why,
we all need a friend along the way.

LAURALYN W. BELLAMY

May the love that overcomes all differences,
    heals all wounds,
    puts to flight all fears,
    reconciles all who are separated
be in us and among us, now and always.

FREDERICK E. GILLIS

Be ye lamps unto yourselves; be your own confidence.
Hold to the truth within yourselves as to the only lamp.

BUDDHIST

Benediction

May our hearts rejoice in heavenly mirth, being set at liberty,
established in gentleness, enduring in charity, surprised by joy.

JOHN F. HAYWARD

Be ours a religion which, like sunshine, goes everywhere:
    its temple, all space;
    its shrine, the good heart;
    its creed, all truth;
    its ritual, works of love;
    its profession of faith, divine living.

THEODORE PARKER

With faith to face our challenges,
with love that casts out fear,
with hope to trust tomorrow,
we accept this day as the gift it is:
    a reason for rejoicing.

GARY KOWALSKI

O Spinner, Weaver, Seamstress of our lives,
your loom is love.
May we be empowered by that love
to weave new patterns of truth and justice
into a web of life that is strong, beautiful, and everlasting.

BARBARA WELLS

As we leave this community of the spirit,
may we remember the difficult lesson
that each day offers more things than we can do.
May we do what needs to be done,
postpone what does not,
and be at peace with what we can be and do.
Therefore, may we learn to separate
that which matters most
from that which matters least of all.

RICHARD S. GILBERT

Reminded that we are part and participants of the universe, let
us go forth from the quiet of this hour, encouraged to strive
toward faithfulness to the best in ourselves, in others, and in all
of creation.

NORMAN V. NAYLOR

Beauty is before me, and beauty behind me.
Above me and below me hovers the beautiful.
I am surrounded by it; I am immersed in it.
In my youth, I am aware of it,
and, in old age, I shall walk quietly the beautiful trail.
In beauty it is begun. In beauty it is ended.

FROM THE NAVAJO

We receive fragments of holiness, glimpses of eternity,
    brief moments of insight.
Let us gather them up for the precious gifts that they are,
    and, renewed by their grace, move boldly into the unknown.

SARA MOORES CAMPBELL

May we never rest until every child of earth in every generation
    is free from all prisons of the mind
    and of the body
    and of the spirit,
until the earth and the hills and the seas shall dance
    and the universe itself resound with the joyful cry:
    Behold! I am!

JOHN CUMMINS

In our lives, may we know the holy meaning—the mystery—that
    breaks in at every moment.
May we live at peace with our world and at peace with ourselves,
and may the love of truth guide us in our every day.

MARK MOSHER DeWOLFE

May we follow the path of faith and love this day and in all our
days to come.

ALAN G. DEALE

If, here, you have found freedom,
    take it with you into the world.
If you have found comfort,
    go and share it with others.
If you have dreamed dreams,
    help one another, that they may come true!
If you have known love,
    give some back to a bruised and hurting world.
Go in peace.

LAURALYN BELLAMY

We have a calling in this world:
    we are called to honor diversity,
    to respect differences with dignity,
    and to challenge those who would forbid it.
We are people of a wide path.
Let us be wide in affection
    and go our way in peace.

JEAN M. RICKARD ROWE

Between the dawn and dark of our being, let us be brave and
loving. In our little passage through the light, let us sustain and
forward the human venture—in gentleness, in service, and in
thought.

CARL SEABURG

Our time together ends.
In the days before we come together again,
may our actions match our words,
may our thoughts be filled with love,
and may we truly make a difference in a troubled world.

JIM WICKMAN

Do justly this day and all days.
Be of goodwill.
Walk humbly before the mysteries of life
and before that gulf which separates us from the ideals we
    profess.
Live in peace and praise.
Our day is just beginning.
So be it.

ELLEN JOHNSON-FAY

Take courage, friends.
    The way is often hard,
    the path is never clear,
    and the stakes are very high.
Take courage, for deep down there is another truth:
    You are not alone.

WAYNE B. ARNASON

May the patience that makes life tolerable,
    the laughter that eases pain,
    the reverence that makes life holy, and
    the love that is God
be with us now and in every time.

MAX A. COOTS

Remembering that the universe is so much larger
    than our ability to comprehend,
let us go forth from this time together with the resolve
    to stop trying to reduce the incomprehensible
    to our own petty expectations,
so that wonder, that sense of what is sacred,
    can open up our minds
    and light up our lives.

MARJORIE NEWLIN LEAMING

For Seasonal Celebrations and Special Occasions

SPRING/EASTER

May the spirit of life, a gift of the earth's renewal, come awake
inside us again. And may we find it holy!

JUDITH E. MEYER

May we have joy this Easter, a joy born of life well lived;
may we have love this Easter, a love stronger than death,
    bringing healing and new growth to our lives;
and may we have peace this Easter, peace that allows us
    to be open to the newness of the season
    and gives us reason to sing.

JUDITH G. MANNHEIM

Now let us go forth with the faith that life is worth living, that
defeat and adversity can be transformed into victory and hope,
that love is eternal, and that life is stronger than death.

And may that faith inspire us to live our lives with dignity, love,
and courage in the days and weeks ahead.

WILLIAM R. MURRY

SUMMER

Happiness and summer joys are made of
    peepers breaking the silence of the night,
    mourning doves cooing in the early dawn,
    wildflowers hidden along a forest path,
    and a child presenting a bouquet of dandelions.
It is through such gentle and often quiet nudgings from nature
    that we commune with the sustaining forces of life.
It is through such gentle and quiet communion with family,
        friends, and occasional strangers that we encounter the
        divine.

CHARLES J. STEPHENS

THANKSGIVING

May we be inspired with gratitude for the wondrous gifts
    that are ours
and be filled with the resolve to share them
    with all who are in need.
May we hold precious one another, and the world
    which provides us with sustenance and beauty.
And may a song of thanksgiving be on our lips to the creator
    and sustainer of life.

MARTA M. FLANAGAN

CHRISTMAS

Let us sing the song of angels now, the song of hope, of
    love, of courage, of everlasting exaltation.
May our ears always be open to the voice of angels, to the
    song of the spirit, to the solemnity of solitude.
May our voices never fear to sing out in praise of the birth
    of new life, new hope, and a new future.
So be it.

MICHAEL A. McGEE

May the love of this season be with us through all the days of
the year and give us strength and courage and faith. May the
peace of this season be ever in us and bring us comfort and
hope. May the light of this season shine in our hearts and bring
us happiness and laughter. May the joy that is in us be shared
with others.

KENNETH W. PHIFER

Christmas is for everyone. Christmas touches the child within and awakens us to the joys of times past. Let us also celebrate the present and build memories for the future. Let us go forth with joy.

ROBERTA M. NELSON